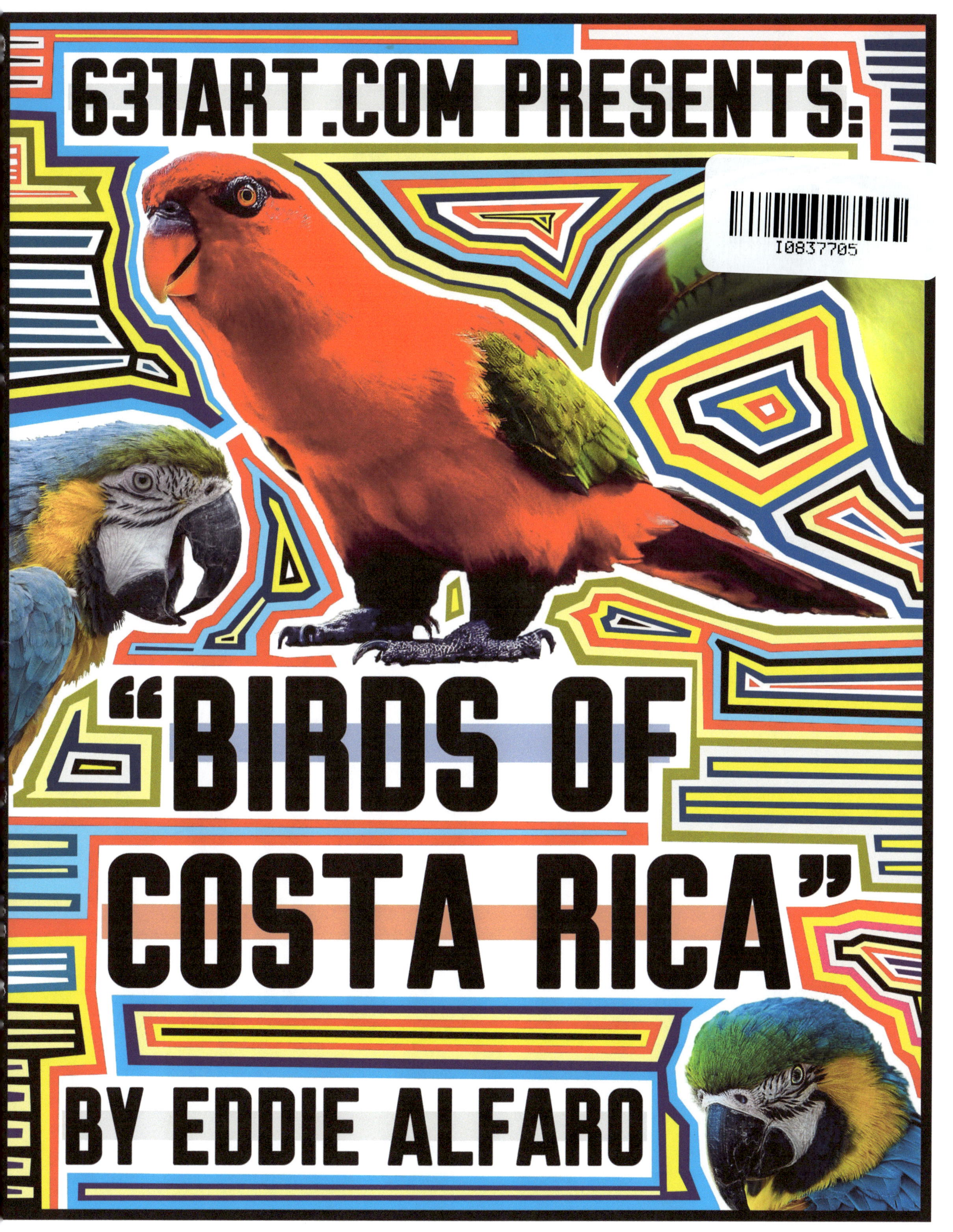

631ART.COM PRESENTS:
"BIRDS OF COSTA RICA"
BY EDDIE ALFARO

CLAY-COLORED THRUSH
THE NATIONAL BIRD
OF COSTA RICA

THE COPPERY-HEADED EMERALD
IS A SMALL HUMMINGBIRD ENDEMIC
TO COSTA RICA. IT MEASURES
ONLY 3 INCHES IN LENGTH, AND
WEIGHS ONLY 0.11 OZ.
COPPERY-HEADED EMERALD

HUMMINGBIRD

THE GREEN-CROWNED BRILLIANT
IS A LARGE HUMMINGBIRD THAT LIVES
IN THE HIGHLANDS OF COSTA RICA.

GREEN-CROWNED BRILLIANT

TANAGERS CONSTRUCT
HOMES ON BRANCHES
AS HIGH AS 75 FEET.
GREEN-HEADED TANAGER

RED-HEADED TROGON

WHITE-CROWNED PIGEONS
CLIMB ABOUT IN TREES
WITH GREAT AGILITY, EVEN
HANGING UPSIDE DOWN.
WHITE-CROWNED PIGEON

SCARLET MACAWS EAT
CLAY FROM RIVERBANKS.
SCIENTISTS ARE NOT SURE
WHY THEY DO THIS.

SCARLET MACAW

BICOLOURED HAWK

TOUCAN'S TAKE SHELTER IN
HOLLOWED OUT TREES USUALLY
CREATED BY WOODPECKERS.
TOUCAN

GREAT GREEN
MACAW

IN FLIGHT, THE LONG TAIL OF THE GROOVE-BILLED ANI, SWINGS UP AND DOWN AND FROM SIDE TO SIDE LIKE A PENDULUM.
GROOVE-BILLED ANI

FIERY-BILLED
ARACARI

OROPENDOLA LIVE IN COLONIES OF ABOUT 30 NESTS, EACH COLONY HAS A DOMINANT MALE WHICH MATES WITH MOST OF THE FEMALES.
OROPENDOLA

NEW WORLD WARBLER

MOTMOTS OFTEN MOVE
THEIR TAIL BACK AND FORTH
IN A WAG-DISPLAY WHEN
THEY DETECT PREDATORS.
MOTMOT

CHESTNUT-MANDIBLED TOUCAN

BLACK VULTURES ARE ABLE
TO EAT DISEASED MEAT
WITHOUT GETTING ILL.
BLACK VULTURE

WREN

THE GRAY-LINED HAWK
IS FOUND FROM SOUTHERN
COSTA RICA TO ARGENTINA.
GRAY-LINED HAWK

PLAIN CHACHALACA

KINGFISHERS HAVE EXCELLENT VISION AND CAN SEE INTO WATER, EVEN ADJUSTING FOR REFRACTION.
KINGFISHER

YELLOW-EARED TOUCANET

THE NAME "KISKADEE" REFERS TO THE "KIS-KA-DEE" CALLS, THAT GREAT KISKADEE OFTEN PRODUCES.
GREAT KISKADEE

ANTBIRD

THREE-WATTLED BELLBIRD
THE THREE-WATTLED BELLBIRD IS NAMED FOR THE MALE'S THREE SKINNY, EXTENDED WORM-LOOKING SKIN STRUCTURES WHICH HANG FROM HIS BILL.

THE
END.
THANK
YOU.

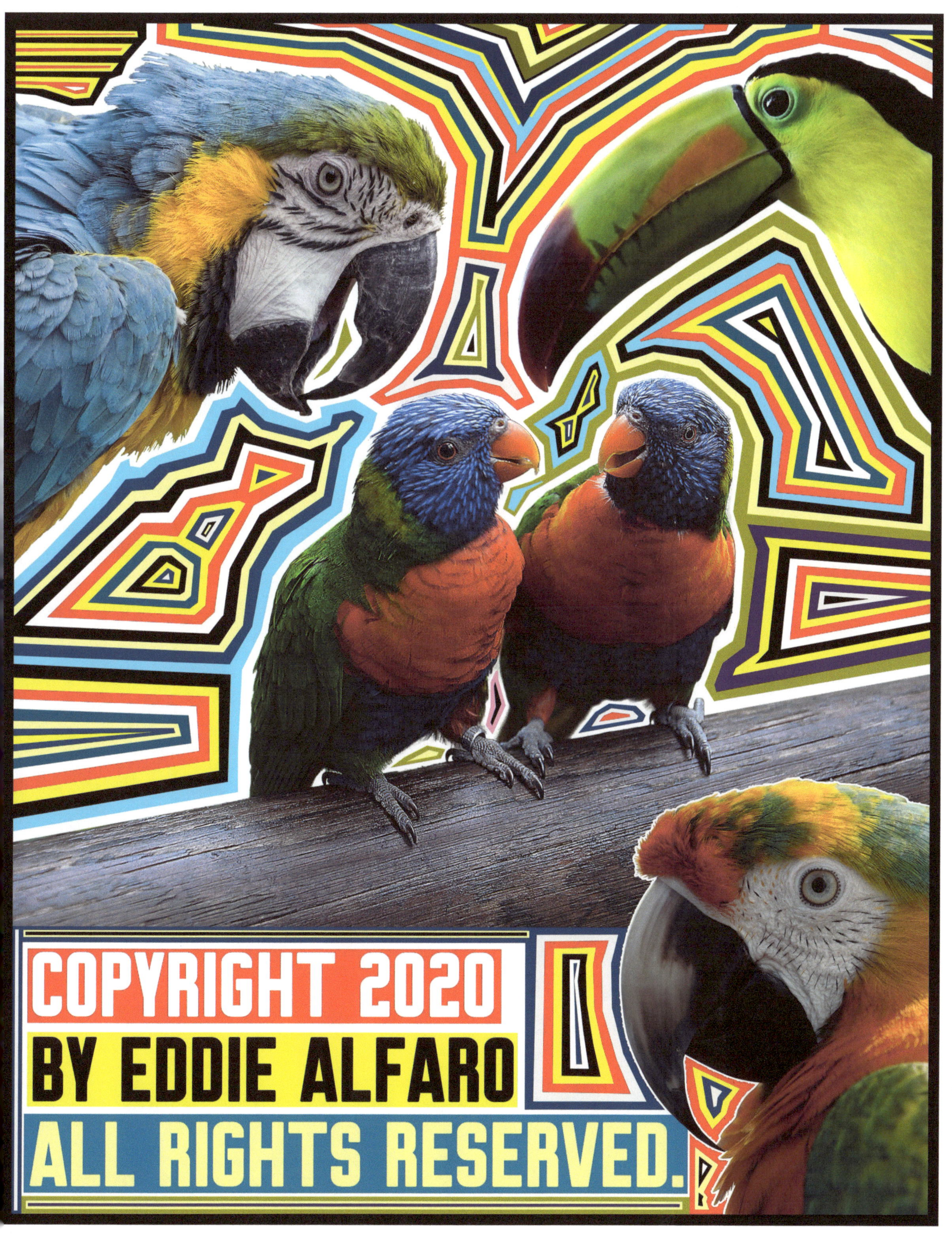
COPYRIGHT 2020
BY EDDIE ALFARO
ALL RIGHTS RESERVED.

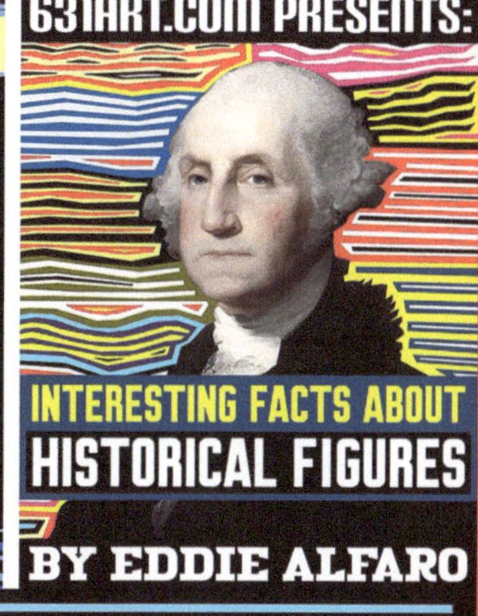

MORE BOOKS AT:

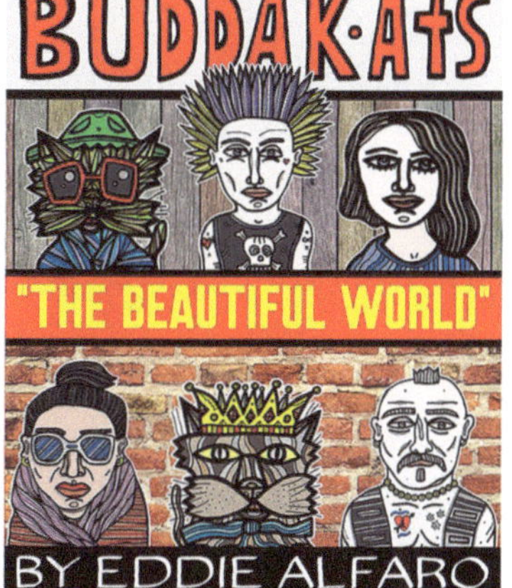

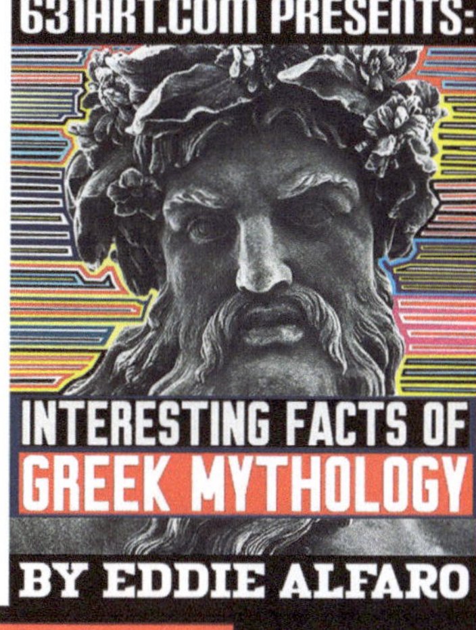

631ART.COM

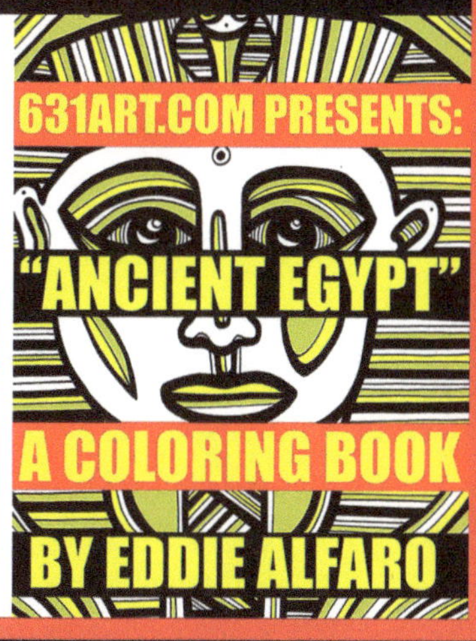